A HEROINE'S JOURNAL
Healing the Inner Child

CHERYL FRANCIS

A HEROINE'S JOURNAL
www.highvibrationlevel.com

ISBN: 978-1-77277-431-3

References to internet websites (URLs) were accurate at the time of writing. Authors and the publishers are not responsible for URLs that may have expired or changed since the manuscript was prepared.

Limits of Liability and Disclaimer of Warranty

The author and publisher shall not be liable for your misuse of the enclosed material. This book is strictly for informational and educational purposes only.

Warning – Disclaimer

The purpose of this journal is to educate and entertain. The author and/or publisher do not guarantee that anyone following these techniques, suggestions, tips, ideas, or strategies will become successful. The author and/or publisher shall have neither liability nor responsibility to anyone with respect to any loss or damage caused, or alleged to be caused, directly or indirectly by the information contained in this book.

Medical Disclaimer

The medical or health information in this journal is provided as an information resource only, and is not to be used or relied on for any diagnostic or treatment purposes. This information is not intended to be patient education, does not create any patient-physician relationship, and should not be used as a substitute for professional diagnosis and treatment.

Publisher
10-10-10 Publishing
Markham, ON
Canada
Printed in Canada and the United States of America

Dear Reader……

Thank you for trusting me with your time to take this journey with me as you go within to heal the Inner Child. It is worth noting that throughout the process while clearing and healing the Chakras certain traumas and wounding may rise to the surface. Therefore during these times because the pain and fear is so great you might be tempted to forfeit the journey. Please don't give up; trust and believe that this process is all part of the journey to healing and greatness.

When the pain from the past surfaces take some deep breaths to relax the body. Remember our pains and traumas are stored in the DNA and chakras of the body. The ego wants to forget what happened don't allow it. It is in confronting the pain that healing can begin.

Let's get started with a prayer. Remember to be gentle with yourself.

Good luck on your journey to transformation.

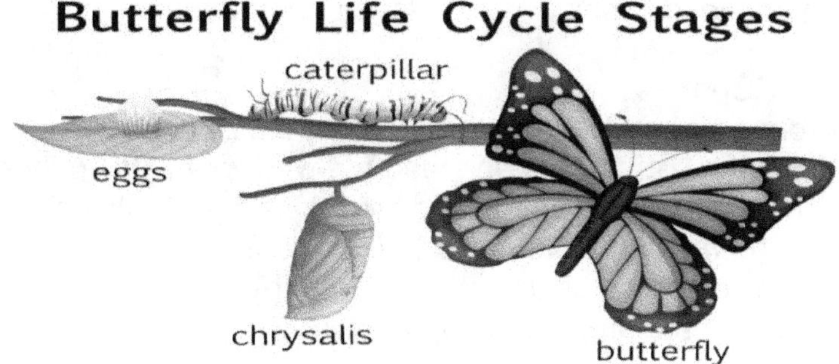

PRAYER TO BREAK A SOUL TIE & TRAUMA BOND

Dear God,
Cleanse me with your divine love and propel me to greatness. Bring back my power and cleanse my energy field with pure light. I thank you for the precious gift of life. I thank you that you have blessed me with a second chance to continue witnessing your glory. I am greatful that you have brought me this far. I am greatful that you have blessed me with the experience to understand the difference between light and darkness and from now onwards I choose to follow the path of pure light. I forgive myself for the hurtful and painful experience I have been through during these previous relationships. I now allow myself to heal and fully recover into a healthy beautiful soul that I am meant to be. I now allow my soul to shine, so bright that it brings down the shadows of evil and darkness the enemy has built around my being. I break the dark energy that the enemy has used to bond my soul with theirs during the friendships and/or relationships. From now onwards I am breaking the soul ties, and trauma bonds and all previous energies from my toxic family members, bosses and friends, that are not of my highest good. I now release them and forgive them and from now on I choose to shine in pure love and greatness.

Dear God,
From now on, drive me torwards my life purpose.
Clear the path for me and lead me with your light so that I can follow the journey that is meant for me. Continue healing me and as I recover, align me with the right person worthy of my precious love. I am worthy of love, I am worthy of restored health, I am worthy of divine abundance. With this prayer, I know it is already done.

AMEN
By Denzo Mos - Youtuber

Stage 1: Departure

PART 1:

ACCEPTANCE

Today I accept myself and others and will take the following steps to exhibit this in my daily life.

PART 2:

GRATITUDE

Today I am grateful for.

Stage 2: Initiation

PART 3:

LET GO AND LET GOD

Today I let go of my past and allow God to take away my trauma and pain.

PART 4:

PHEONIX RISING

Today I forgive myself and others as I rise from the ashes.

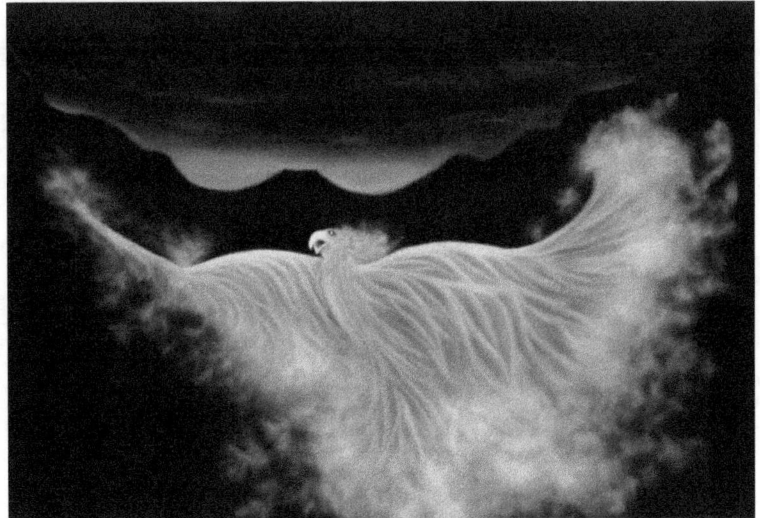

PART 5:

MEDITATION

Today I go within and balance my chakras.

PART 6:

UNION WITH SELF

Today I do the necessary shadow work.

Stage 3: Return

PART 7:

SELF ACTUALIZATION

Today I identify my purpose.

PART 8:

MANIFESTATION

Today I write and speak my intentions.

PART 9:

PURPOSE

Today I bring my purpose into reality.

PART 10:

ROLL OUT OF THE PLAN

Today I use my healing to help others.

www.ingramcontent.com/pod-product-compliance
Lightning Source LLC
LaVergne TN
LVHW020654100826
845148LV00012B/2481